The National Gallery
Booklover's Book

The National Gallery

Booklover's Book

NATIONAL
GALLERY

National Gallery Publications Limited 1993

Reprinted 1994, 1996

NGPL Stock Number 301012
ISBN 1 85709 034 9

Typographic design by Peter Guy

Printed and bound in Great Britain
by Butler and Tanner Limited, Frome and London

Contents

"Go, little book, and wish to all
Flowers in the garden, meat in the hall,
A bin of wine, a spice of wit,
a house with lawn enclosing it,
a living river by the door,
a nightingale in the sycamore."

Book 1 *Envoy*
Robert Louis Stevenson
(1850-1894)

Books to buy

Books to buy

Books to buy

Books to buy

Books to buy

Books to buy

Books to buy

Books to buy

Books to buy

Books to buy

Books to buy

Books to borrow from a library

Books to borrow from a library

Books to borrow from a library

Books to borrow from a library

Books to borrow from a library

Books to borrow from a library

Books to borrow from a library

Books to borrow from a library

Books to borrow from a library

Books to borrow from a library

Books to borrow from a library

Books borrowed from friends

Books borrowed from friends

Books borrowed from friends

Books borrowed from friends

Books borrowed from friends

Books borrowed from friends

B*ooks borrowed from friends*

Books borrowed from friends

Books borrowed from friends

Books borrowed from friends

Books borrowed from friends

Books lent

Books lent

Books lent

Books lent

Books lent

Books lent

Books lent

50

Books lent

Books lent

Books lent

Books lent

Books by category

Books by category

Books by category

Books by category

59

Books by category

Books by category

Books by category

Books by category

Books by category

Books by category

Books by category

Books for children

Books for children

Books for children

Books *for children*

Books for children

Books for children

Books for children

Books for children

Books *for children*

Books for children

Books for children

Books to give

Books to give

Books to give

Books to give

Books to give

Books to give

Books to give

Books to give

Books to give

Books to give

Books read

Books read

Books read

Books read

Books read

Books read

Books read

Books read

Books read

Books read

Books read

Notes

Notes

Notes

Notes

Notes

Notes

Notes

List of illustrations

List of illustrations: continued